Th

Guide To

Behaviour

Shelly Newstead

The Buskers Guide to Behaviour

ISBN - 1-904792-14-6
© Shelly Newstead 2005

Illustrations © Chris Bennett 2005

Published by Common Threads Publications Ltd.
Wessex House
Upper Market Street
Eastleigh
Hampshire SO50 9FD.
T: 07000 785215
E: info@commonthreads.co.uk

Other titles in The Buskers Guide series include;
The Buskers Guide to Playing Out
The Buskers Guide to Inclusion
The Buskers Guide to Playwork
The Buskers Guide to Anti-Discriminatory Practice

The text of 'The Buskers Guide...' series can be made available in 14 point font – please contact the publishers by telephoning 07000 785215 or emailing info@commonthreads.co.uk

The Buskers Guide to Behaviour

Contents

Introduction   **page 2**

Chapter 1   **Adults and Behaviour**   **page 9**

Chapter 2   **Fixing the Goalposts**   **page 29**

Chapter 3   **Help - I need somebody ...**   **page 49**

And finally...   **page 70**

Introduction

'Behaviour' is a word that's much bandied about in the field of working with children. Adults go on 'behaviour training', settings ask for 'behaviour consultancy' or for help with their 'behaviour policies'. Some settings have 'behaviour contracts' with children. At the time of writing, even the Government has got in on the act with 'behaviour in schools' becoming a hot topic, not to mention ASBO's and countless other 'behaviour-related' initiatives.

I have to share this with you right away – when I hear anybody talking about 'behaviour' in relation to children, be it professional, parent or politician, my heart sinks. Because 99% of the time, what they are actually talking about is 'bad' behaviour, and they are usually talking about it in a way that implies that there is a problem to be 'fixed'. And that problem generally manifests itself in the shape of a child. The adult starting point generally seems to be 'child-behaviour-trouble-*action stations*'. It's a very 'glass-half-empty' perspective rather than 'glass half-full'.

People go on 'behaviour training' to find out what to do to stop little Johnny kicking the table, or they draw up reams and reams of paperwork so that staff have clear guidance on the 'steps' to 'manage' a child's 'behaviour', as if simply following the instructions on the paperwork will produce the desired results. Presumably the logic behind these procedures is that when the desired results have been produced, we can stop talking (and thinking) about 'behaviour' again. Short-term, problem-focussed thinking which gets us nowhere.

Because the trouble is, of course, that things just aren't that simple. Children, like the rest of the human race, are generally complex beings, with emotions and motivations that are individual to them. In a setting of 40 children, you will find 40 different little packages of thought patterns, range of reactions, background influences and intrinsic desires, plus, of course, the individual packages that the adults in that setting bring with them too. Mix these all up, and I hope you'll start to get the gist of why a 'five step plan to behaviour management' is quite unlikely to get us very far. But when the 'five step plan' (or whatever) fails, what do adults do then?

Well, in my experience they come on training courses and ask me, and the conversation then goes something like this....

'I don't know.'
'But you must do — you're the behaviour trainer.'
'Sorry, it isn't that simple.'
'But what's the point of coming on a training course if we don't go home with the answer?'

The answer, of course, is that there is no 'answer', only approaches, to 'behaviour.' Following a 'behaviour policy' might help adults to feel more in control once we are going through the process, but once we get to the end of it, it leaves neither us, nor the child, any options. And what do we do once the 'plan' hasn't worked? We panic – stigmatise the child (who has already probably got so many labels and stickers and star charts that nobody could ever hope to ignore the fact that she's the one with the 'problem'), phone the parents, call in the consultant. It's very easy to forget that, at the start of the process, there was a child, who might very well have had a problem, although by now it probably isn't the one you thought she had to start with. As the process of 'behaviour management' continues, so the child (along with her original problem) becomes further and further entrenched in a process that only seems to compound her distress rather than to help her to get out of it. We put children through 'the behaviour mangle' and then stand back in amazement when they come out the other end even more emotionally battered and bruised than they started.

The difficulty with 'behaviour management' is that these procedures seem to take on a life of their own and lose the child sight of the child. The cry from adults rarely seems to be, 'This child is in trouble, how can we help?' but rather, 'What do we do next (to make her 'behave')?'

I hear all the time about 'star charts' that don't produce the desired results, rules that the kids have made (in accordance with the latest 'good wisdom' from somewhere or other) being broken by the children themselves, and 'strategies' for 'managing children's behaviour' which sounded like such a good idea at the time but...

These 'techniques' do not 'work' (that is, produce the desired effects) most of the time because of one simple fact, which is this...In all of this flummery, trickery and downright bribery of children, we adults not only get sidetracked away from relating to the child, we also forget one simple truth – we are the adults. It is us who need to take responsibility, we who need to establish boundaries and to support children, we who need to build and maintain rapport and build children's self-esteem. In other words, we need to take children's behaviour (in all its glory) to heart more. Instead of pushing children away, hiding behind policies, procedures and protocols, we need to be saying to ourselves and the children, 'We all have a responsibility here, let's work out how we get it right.' And that, for us, means thinking about how we approach 'behaviour' and whether our approach is actually going to help the children we work with to take their share of responsibility too.

So we need a new way of thinking about 'behaviour', because the 'answer' to any 'behaviour issue' is not 'out there somewhere', it's not in any book (including this one), neither is it on the (normally very informative) world wide web. And that's what this book is about – finding a new perspective from which adults can think about children's behaviour and their responses to it. Because any solution, if such a thing exists at all, can only be found by asking the right question – and at the time of writing it seems to me that most adults are not even speaking the right language, let alone asking the right question.

Once adults get a new perspective on behaviour, then we can stop looking for 'the answer' and concentrate on the real purpose of why we get involved in children's behaviour. We can roast the old chestnuts of 'behaviour management' until they shrivel up and disappear, and put into place not new systems, procedures and diktats, but instead a new way of thinking about children's appropriate and inappropriate responses to what goes on around and within them. 'Dealing with children's behaviour' should be a source of great interest, professional curiosity and even joy (yes, really!) for professionals who work with children, setting us challenges on how to meet the needs of the children we work with even better, rather than the doom-laden, overly-policied and over-policed millstone that seems to

engender trouble and strife every working day.
By the end of this book, I can categorically state that
neither you nor I will be able to stop little Johnny from
kicking the table, nor doing anything else for that
matter. But I'm pretty hopeful that you and Johnny will
be getting along a bit better. Approached with a light
heart and positive intentions for the children we work
with, we can make a huge difference not only to the
way that children engage with the wider world, but also
how the wider world engages with them. Let the fun
begin…!

Shelly Newstead

PS: Feedback, as always, is extremely welcome –
please send your comments to
buskersguides@commonthreads.co.uk.
I look forward to hearing from you!

8

Chapter 1
Adults and Behaviour

I expect you've noticed from the title of this chapter that we're actually not going to think about children's behaviour just yet. No, hang on a minute, don't rush off to Chapter 2 - we can't get going on children's behaviour straight away because that's simply not the right place to start. I know this sounds weird, but stay with me a while… You see, we adults need to get our heads round a few things before we even begin to think about the kids. If we don't, not only are we going to end up in a right old muddle, but so are they! (And when that happens you really need to have your head in the right place about 'behaviour' – but that's Chapter 3 already…)

So for all of you who are really keen to get on with finding a way to 'sort out little Johnny's behaviour', I need you to do something for me before we go any further. In a minute, put the book down, close your eyes, get a mental image of 'little Johnny' in your

10

head....and then wave him goodbye and watch him leave your headspace. Then, and only then, when he is well and truly out of the picture, can you think about 'behaviour' – not his behaviour, but behaviour. Believe me, it's more interesting than you think....

Has he gone yet? Just checking....

'Behaviour'?

First things first – we just need to sort out what we mean by this word 'behaviour'. As I said in the introduction, it seems to me that every time you hear an adult talking about 'children's behaviour', it basically means that children are doing something wrong. What a shame!

Why? Well, because it focuses our attention on the negative, the 'bad', the things that need

Psst, I've had my eye on that kid for ages... so far he's done absolutely nothing wrong but I'm sure... any minute now...

'sorting'. And guess what we see if that's what we're looking for? Yep, you've got it – we spot loads of negatives, oodles of 'bad' stuff and just heaps of things that need sorting. Not only does this irritate the children we work with (and let's face it, grumpy children can't generally be relied on to produce their best behaviour), but it also winds us adults up, which in turn stresses out the kids again, which then results in......you guessed it, a self-fulfilling prophecy.

So let's get this word pinned down before we go any further. 'Behaviour' really just means the way we act, or how we go about things. And the way we act can have good and bad consequences for us, other people and the world around us. In other words, 'behaviour' is simply the word that describes the 'doing' bit of human beings.

So when we're working with children we've got to resist the temptation of focussing on the negatives - 'behaviour' does not mean 'bad behaviour', it just means 'doing stuff.' When we talk about 'children's behaviour', we should be talking about 'what children do', rather than 'the stuff that needs sorting out'. So from now on in this book, when you see the word 'behaviour', I'd like you to make sure that your brain is thinking 'how we act', not 'bad stuff'. It will help, honest!

Why do adults get involved?

Why adults get involved in children's behaviour seems to be a really important question that either doesn't get asked or appears to be very difficult to answer. Ask yourself the question now and see what you come up with…..Do your thoughts look anything like this list?

❖ to get children to behave properly
❖ to stop children hurting themselves or each other
❖ to teach them right from wrong
❖ to teach them manners.

These are all pretty common answers and I guess that it could be argued that there's a grain of truth in all of them. But if this is the whole answer as to why adults should get involved in children's behaviour, then we've got a problem.

Why? Well, if you take another look at the list, you will probably notice that they are all pretty negative. There is an underlying assumption there that children won't 'behave properly' unless we get involved, or that children will hurt themselves or each other if we're not there to sort stuff out, for example. They seem to imply that children need constant adult supervision and intervention, otherwise it will all go horribly wrong. We know that this is not the case – in fact, some would argue that it will all go horribly wrong for children if we are constantly sorting their lives out when they could get on with it themselves!

We've also got a problem with the last two – just whose version of right or wrong, or whose idea of 'manners' are we teaching them? And what happens if that person's values in those areas clash with the child's or the families' values? And what exactly do we mean by 'behaving properly' anyway? You see, unless we have a clear reason for getting involved in children's behaviour, we start to stray into all sorts of murky areas which can work against us....

So let's make it simple for adults and children alike – the reason that we get involved in children's behaviour is to help children to act in a way which will meet the expectations of the setting. (I know that this raises the question of what are the expectations of the setting, but have no fear, we'll get to that in Chapter 2!) So now we have a positive purpose for getting involved in children's behaviour and positive intentions towards children's behaviour - that is, we are helping children to meet expectations, rather than stopping them from producing unacceptable behaviours. Feels better already, doesn't it?!

By the way, it's important for adults to recognise that, unless settings have very specific behavioural agendas for children, we can't hope to influence children's behaviour outside the setting. Children are perfectly able to live in a world where there are different sets of

14

rules for different places they find themselves, and we need to respect other ways of working and being with children that do not reflect the behaviour expectations of our setting. So children in out-of-school clubs which take place in schools, for example, can understand that they can't run in the corridors during the day when there are hundreds of children around, but it's fine in the evenings when there's not so many. We need to give children credit for being able to understand reasonable and realistic expectations – it's the unreasonable and unrealistic ones that they have problems with!

Common sense?

Adults have all sorts of ideas about 'behaviour'. What's right and wrong, what should be 'done' about behaviour, what should and shouldn't be said to children about behaviour, what 'works' and what doesn't…Which is great, because at least it shows that everybody is thinking about it. But the trouble with everybody thinking about is that the majority of us are all thinking about it slightly differently.

Now this happens for all sorts of reasons – we were all brought up differently, for a start, which means that we all have different expectations about behaviour. And some of us have our own children, and we have a set of expectations about their behaviour. Different types of settings can approach things differently, and we also get different 'trends' in practice.

This potential hotchpotch of values, beliefs and practice isn't a problem – until, of course, we all start working in one setting. As individuals, we all tend to think that our approach is 'common sense', because that's what it feels like to us – and of course it would do, because our values and the way we go about acting on them are very much part of us. But if we think about it logically, we know that 'common sense' can't exist – because what's 'common' about 'common sense' isn't actually 'common', and if it were, then we'd all think the same – and we don't. (Sorry about that – please feel free to go back and read that sentence again!)

Whose line is it anyway?

The other difficulty with our various ideas about behaviour is that it isn't fair to assume that our values coincide with the values of the children and families that we work with. It might be 'common sense' in your family, for example, to always say 'please' and 'thank you', but that won't be the same in every family. And who's to say which way of behaving is 'right'? Our personal values and beliefs are really important to us as individuals, but we can't use them to help us establish professional expectations of children's behaviour in our settings. We need to base our professional practice on fair and realistic expectations of the children we work with, rather than our personal ideals.

And just in case I haven't convinced you on this one yet, try thinking about it this way. By insisting on certain specific types of behaviour in our settings which are not realistic for children, we may well be setting them up to fail. Children may never be able to meet our inappropriate expectations, so to carry on insisting that they try is only going to increase the child's chances of getting it wrong. And children who get stuff wrong all the time tend to have bad self-esteem. And bad self-esteem is more likely to lead to 'bad' behaviour…starting to sound like we're shooting ourselves in the foot with this one, doesn't it?!

When do we get involved?

Now here's where it starts getting a bit more complicated. If we think back to earlier in the chapter, when we said that 'behaviour' simply means 'the way we act', then we can see that 'behaviour' in itself is value-free. In other words, we can't automatically make a judgement about whether something a child does is positive or negative simply based on an action alone.

For example, 'shouting' is a behaviour. But shouting in itself isn't a good or a bad thing – we can only decide that when we know what is likely to happen as a result of the shouting. And what happens as a result of the shouting will depend on the circumstances in which it takes place. So a child shouting to their mates to pass them the ball during a game of football is not going to cause us any concern. Shouting because you're stuck at the top of a climbing frame and need help is generally a behaviour which we would encourage. But one child shouting down another child's ear to wind them up is a behaviour which is not going to be so well-received. In other words, it's the *effect* of behaviour that we need to be interested in, rather than just the actions themselves.

We weren't shouting. We were playing Mummies and daddies and we were having what my daddy calls "a discussion".

Oh yes, just need to say here before we move on that when we talk about 'effects', we also of course mean 'potential effects' – I'm not for one minute suggesting that you wait for a child to get stabbed with a pair of scissors before you make a judgement about whether that's a good thing or not! We'll get to that in more detail in Chapter 2, but for now I need you to hold on to the idea that us adults need to move away from over-simplified concepts such as 'shouting/spitting/swearing/hitting = 'bad behaviour' – because they're not always.

'Behaviour management'?

'Behaviour management' can be summed up as the traditional way of thinking about behaviour in the field of working with children. The phrase has come to mean something like 'putting a stop to/curing/sorting out negative behaviours and getting children to produce only the types of behaviours we want to see in the setting'. It seems to imply that adults can (and should) make children conform to the required forms of behaviour, which in turn suggests that there are specific ways of achieving this.

This then sends everybody on 'behaviour management' courses searching for the holy grail of behaviour – but don't get me started on that one again, we'll never get out of Chapter 1... (If you missed my rant on this, please feel free to go back to the introduction at this point – I would hate you to have missed it...) However, I must just tell you one thing here. If the holy grail of behaviour did exist, if there really was one sure-fire way of stopping kids from producing the type of behaviour that isn't acceptable in the setting - do you think I'd still be here? Nope, absolutely not – 'cos I'd have found it, copyrighted it, slapped a patent on it, sold it to squillions of professionals (and parents!) and be half-way round the world on my luxury yacht by now!

Contrary to the hard and fast principles of 'behaviour management', there is no process or procedure that adults can follow to 'make children behave'. The word 'management' implies control, getting results, making sure that things turn out as they should do. There are lots of things we can – and should – manage in our settings. We manage hazards so that children are exposed to an appropriate level of risk, and we manage projects such as trips or special events, so that things go (more or less) according to plan and everybody has a good time. 'Management' isn't therefore a bad thing in our line of work – it just isn't the right style of behaviour for adults to adopt when it comes to getting involved with children's behaviour.

This is because we can't hope to 'manage' children's behaviour in the way that we would manage other areas of our settings. Nobody can make anybody else behave in a certain way. I don't want to go all psychological on you, but it is true, is it not, that the only person who can change any way in which they behave is the person themselves? No amount of bribery, cajoling or pleading will get anybody (child or adult) to change their behaviour unless they have really made up their own minds to do so. So to imply that adults can make

where's step 6?

children change the way that they behave by a process of 'management' is really leading us up the garden path.

There you go then - 'behaviour management' is a load of old tripe. (Oh, I've been dying to see that in print for years!) There are no special skills, no set procedures or processes which will tell us how to make children do the things we want them to do (and some would argue that this is a very good thing). We can't manage children like we manage budgets. And once adults can accept that, everybody's lives (including – and especially – the children's) get a whole lot easier.

Leadership, not management

Now at this point on training courses, people generally put their heads in their hands and whimper, saying things like, 'Does that mean that if we get rid of the 'behaviour management' strategies, rip up the star charts and banish the sticky dinosaurs that we are going to be left with a great gaping vacuum which can only lead to anarchy?'

The answer to that question is yes – and no. Yes, it's true, by the end of this book I would like you to go out and put the 'behaviour charts' and the smiley dinosaurs (cute as they are) and any other form of 'behaviour bribery' on the bonfire to roast along with the rest of the old chestnuts. (I'll tell you why in Chapter 3!) But no, it doesn't mean that the only thing we're left with is an 'anything goes' approach which will lead to chaos and anarchy – far from it.

Because (and I hope you'll forgive me for stating the obvious here) children are – well, children - and they are learning about behaviour every day as they grow up. There are all sorts of ways of behaving ('social codes' if you like) that are not immediately obvious to children, and sometimes these social codes conflict, which make

them even more difficult for children to get their heads round. So children need support and guidance from all the adults in their lives to help them to understand what is appropriate behaviour in the various situations they find themselves. Adults are adults, and we rule the world because children can't – they simply don't have the knowledge, skills or necessary abilities yet. So children need boundaries, rules, limits - however you want to put it, children need to know what (and where) the bottom line is.

But the way that adults need to provide that support and guidance is by working with the child. Not through a medium of a policy or set procedure, but through an honest and open relationship that wants the child to succeed (remember positive intentions and positive purpose?). Because once we accept the fact that there is no holy grail, no one answer to make a child behave in a certain way, we can stop wasting our time and energy trying to make our 'five-step-plan-to-angeldom-one-punishment-cures-all' behaviour policy work (when in our heart of hearts we know it has severe limitations). Instead of reaching for the restrictive framework of policies and procedures and strategies, we need to provide an open and constructive space within which we can work with the child to help them to achieve the expectations of the setting. This does not, of course, guarantee that they will achieve it, but it does mean that they have a better chance of doing so because we've started with a positive intention, rather than a negative one.

Or to put it another way, what we need to focus on is behaviour leadership, rather than behaviour management. 'Leadership' is about motivating people and working with others to facilitate some sort of change. 'Management' is about following a set of procedures which (barring the unforeseens) more or less guarantee you the outcome you set out to achieve, whilst leadership is about adopting a more flexible approach to enable other people to achieve the change with you. 'Behaviour management' starts with a negative focus ('I'm going to put a stop to this once and for all') and 'behaviour leadership' begins with a positive intention ('Ok, we've got a problem here – how are we going to solve it?').

Now, would you like the good news or the bad news first? Let's start with the bad – ah, caught you out did I, you thought I was going for the tried-and-tested method of good stuff first to soften the blow of the bad stuff? Sorry, never been a believer in that particular pearl of wisdom – mainly because it's so often used that now you can't tell anybody anything good without them panicking about what's going to come next! Anyway, the bad news, here it is. Behaviour leadership is harder

25

work for adults than behaviour management. And the good news? Behaviour leadership is far more effective and far less stressful way of working with children than behaviour management – both for adults and children. Basically, it's much easier to try to 'control and contain' children's behaviour by operating a series of set procedures, because it takes less energy and less brain power than thinking about the child in front of us and the range of responses that might help them. (Even if we know it's not going to work, in behaviour management after Step 2 comes Step 3, and somehow that's far more comforting than some empty space that promises no answers...) So, if it would help at this point, here's what we need to do to be behaviour leaders rather than behaviour managers;

1. understand the reason for getting involved in children's behaviour and intervene only on that basis
2. have realistic and unambiguous expectations about childrens' behaviour in the setting
3. help children to meet those expectations

I hope you've spotted from that list that behaviour leadership is about us – what we do and how we think about children and their behaviour. One of the biggest problems of 'behaviour management' is that it encourages us to start putting children through the behaviour mangle without taking a long, hard look at what we're doing first. So by the end of this book, I hope you'll all be confident behaviour leaders, working flexibly with children to help them to stick to the behaviour expectations in your setting, rather than frustrated behaviour managers, following rigid procedures that have nothing to do with the child in front of you who is struggling. But before we march on into Chapter 2, let's just check that we're all happy with this idea of behaviour leadership.

Behaviour leadership

'Behaviour' means the way we act, and the way we act can have positive or negative results. Adults working with children get involved in behaviour to help children meet the expectations in the setting, and these expectations must be realistic for the children we are working with, rather than being rooted in our own personal values. It is the effect (or the potential effect) of behaviour that adults need to make judgements about, rather than a behaviour itself. Behaviour leadership requires adults to take responsibility for helping a child to change their behaviour through a range of strategies which are appropriate to the individual child, whereas behaviour management puts the onus on the child to change through a series of pre-determined steps which are applicable to everybody.

Ok, now we're getting somewhere! Anybody need a cold compress yet?! Well, we've now done step one of the behaviour leadership model (although I'll have to rely on you for the 'putting it into practice' bit!), so Chapter 2 is going to look at step two in more detail – getting those expectations appropriate and clear. So if you haven't quite got your head round behaviour leadership yet, you may need to go and get yourself a cup of tea (or that cold compress if you prefer!) and have another go at this chapter before you move on. Otherwise, those of you who are feeling strong, lead the way…

Chapter 2
Fixing the Goalposts

Even though we put paid to 'behaviour management' in Chapter 1, I promised that I wouldn't abandon you in the middle of chaos. And see, you can trust me – here we are, start of Chapter 2, fixing the goalposts already. (Or establishing the boundaries, setting the rules, making codes of conduct…whatever other rather inadequate phrase we want to use for letting kids know what's expected of them in our setting.) Remember that Captain Chaos does not rule in behaviour leadership – he might come to visit occasionally, but he does not bring his suitcase.

Because as we said earlier, children do need boundaries (as unfashionable as that way of thinking seems to have become in recent years). But it's really not fair to expect children to guess where the goalposts are – or even worse, to let them decide where they are to start with, only to have adults shifting them about when the children aren't looking (been there, done that, had the breakdown…).

So if, at this point, you're getting quite enthusiastic about the dark arts of making rules with children, just stay with me for a bit longer on the behaviour leadership trail – you and I have got a bit more work to do first!

The 'bottom-line'

Before we get anywhere near talking to children about behaviour, we need to have absolutely crystal clear in our minds what our 'bottom line' is. And by this I mean, what sort of behaviour can we really not accept in the setting?

Now at this point we could all no doubt come up with a marvellous list of 'do's' and 'don'ts', couldn't we? We don't like hitting, we don't like swearing, we like children to be polite and play together nicely…but hang on a minute, we can't fix any goalposts with a list like that.

Why not? Well, several reasons. First of all, there's the bit about personal values and the danger of setting children up to fail with unrealistic expectations. And as we also said in Chapter 1, there can't be any 'absolutes' when thinking about behaviour, so we need to think about the (likely) effects of behaviour instead.

To give you another example here as a reminder… Spitting might cause a few of us to curl up our toes in disgust, and if a child spat at another child we might well take a view that that is not on. However, some children with certain medical conditions need to spit – this behaviour in this circumstance is actively encouraged by adults. And if a child spat whilst playing football, copying her favourite football player, would we really make a fuss about that? So 'banning' certain types of behaviour can't be done – otherwise those goalposts will just keep dancing about, depending on the child, the context, the severity of what's happened, etc.

So we need another way of thinking about 'the bottom line'. I think that what we really don't want, if at all avoidable, is children coming to any harm – and harm can, of course, be emotional or physical. So rather than the list of 'do's' and 'don'ts' above, our bottom line sounds something like 'no harm to self, others or property'.

Making judgements

Of course, the fine line between 'likely' and 'actual' harm is a decision that adults alone have to take the responsibility for making. We've all been in situations where, for example, play fighting has gone a bit too far and somebody's got their fingers bent the wrong way (or worse). But then again, we've also all been in situations where playfighting has resulted in no accidents or injuries, helped the children to use up a lot of raw energy and everybody has gone home happy!

Making decisions about whether (or not) to get involved in any sort of behaviour relies on our knowledge of the children, our observation skills and our ability to perform speed-of-light risk assessments. A child who is waving a stick around, for example, may be about to take somebody's eye out with it because they haven't noticed another child close by. We probably would move like greased lightning to try to prevent an accident in this case. Or we may take the decision that the child is well-aware of others around him and the likelihood of harm is extremely limited, so no need to get involved. Waving a stick around does not in itself constitute 'bad' behaviour which automatically requires adult attention. It might be a very important part of the child's game and if at all possible, we adults should

32

therefore leave well alone. We will only be able to make each decision as a result of an on-the-spot risk assessment, rather than always telling children not to wave sticks around in case they might hurt someone.

(It's interesting, isn't it, that so many adult 'rules' are based on the slimmest of chances that children just might do some harm – presumably solely on the basis of them being children – rather than an actual assessment of the likelihood of some sort of harm occurring. For example, 'no ball games' on a patch of open grass – call me odd and call me quirky, but I would have thought that there was much less likelihood of harm coming to anybody than children playing ball games on the open road next to the grass...)

So 'no harm to self, others or property' means that we can focus on the (likely) outcome of a child's behaviour and make a decision based on whether it is actually likely to do any harm. We need to have a consistent approach to getting involved in children's behaviour, rather than confusing the child (and the rest of our team!) by picking up on behaviour which has no (likely) damaging consequences. It's sometimes all too easy for adults to wade in to situations and take over responsibility, whereas in actual fact the child is fully in control and doesn't need the negative attention that they are getting from the adult. Remember, we've shot ourselves in the foot once already in this book, we can't afford to do it again. Children who get negative attention generally feel negative about that, negative feelings could lead them into negative behaviour....so we need to try to make sure that any negative attention is for a real reason, not an imagined one!

Consistency?

So now we really can be consistent about when we get involved in children's behaviour, both in our own individual approach and across our teams. If a behaviour is really likely to cause some harm (physically or emotionally), it's unacceptable in the setting and therefore we need to get involved. If the behaviour is not really likely to cause any harm, then there's no need for us to get involved. Be aware of, sure (just as we are aware of everything that goes on in our setting), keep an eye on from a distance, possibly (if we think the likelihood of harm could increase), but basically leave alone. We discuss this in our team and what we think really might cause harm to children so that we all know when to intervene and when not to. And there we have it - those goalposts are now well and truly fixed.

Sounds simple enough, doesn't it? Ah yes, but then there's the 'adult factor'. Because we adults have a real knack of making life more complicated than it really needs to be – both for ourselves and for the children we work with.

First of all, all those personal values start to creep back in. Remember those from Chapter 1? Things like children needing to learn to say please and thank you, table manners, not shouting 'cos it gives us a headache…etc, etc? Sorry folks, we just can't do it. For all of those very good reasons we've already talked about, it's really not fair on the children to make up our own little set of bye-laws and sub-clauses. We really are just going have to keep those personal values to ourselves to apply them at home, rather than at work.

And then there's that other tried-and-tested adult trick – you know the one. It's called 'moving the goalposts at random'. Imagine the scene…

Johnny wants the keys to the equipment cupboard. He knows that only adults can get stuff out. He's been told 'no' by one of the adults, and that he needs to wait a couple of minutes until someone can help him. So he uses his brain and thinks, 'I might get a different answer from a different adult.' Adult No. 2 originally says no, but after Johnny points out that he has already had that response from somebody else and whines a bit about it, Adult No. 2 gives in and gives him the keys. Finally Johnny can go and get his football – but en route to the cupboard, Adult No. 1 intercepts him, takes the keys away and tells him off for having them in the first place. In addition to which, Adult No. 1 then makes sure that the rest of the adults are made aware that Johnny has been 'devious' in getting the keys and everybody should keep an eye on him from now on.

But hang on a minute! Who broke the rules in the first place? If the rule was no children in the cupboard, why did an adult hand over the key? And far from being 'devious', it could be argued that Johnny was actually performing quite a complicated intellectual feat. Did he get praised for his intellectual prowess? Nope, he just ends up with a 'trouble-maker' label. In other words, Johnny was set up to fail – by adults who broke the rules. Had all the adults stuck to the rules, he would have got a consistent answer – he might not have liked it, but at least he wouldn't have got into trouble for it! (By the way, it's a salutary lesson for us adults to learn - Johnny has probably learnt to go and ask different adults the same question because somewhere along the line, adults have taught him by doing just this that he'll get the right answer...)

Fixing the goalposts for children means that adults

need to respect and maintain those boundaries, regardless of what day of the week it is, how stressed out we're feeling, and even how much children whinge. If we are not consistent, then children cannot be expected to understand what sort of behaviours are or are not acceptable in the setting. Or in other words, the more we move the goalposts, the less chance children have of knowing where they are. Remember, our reason for getting involved in children's behaviour is to help them to understand the expectations of the setting - so why would we want to keep moving the goalposts?

First rule of kids club - We don't sit on the tables.

A quick reality check...

Sometimes groups of adults can find that we've got ourselves into positions which are actually unrealistic or unreasonable when it comes to 'rules'. For example, I often hear in after-school clubs that children are not allowed to help themselves to equipment from the cupboards. The reason often seems to be something to do with the perceived fact that children may do themselves harm (or indeed do some harm) whilst getting stuff to play with out of the cupboards. There may indeed be some places where this is actually the case, although I have to say that I have yet to find one.

You see, in a normal everyday after school club, my speed-of-light risk assessment would probably go something like this...Children who cannot get easy access to equipment they need get bored and frustrated. Many children who are bored and frustrated find it hard to contain those feelings. If those feelings manifest themselves as behaviour then it's not likely to be the sorts of behaviour that adults (or other children) might appreciate. If I allow access to the cupboard, the most harm that could happen is that we might need to tidy it up every now and again. If I don't....ooops, there goes my other foot!

Sometimes it seems to me that rules just 'are', rather than having any logical thought behind them. For example, in an after school session, when the children have come straight in from a long day in school, is it realistic to expect them to sit still and quiet for registration for half an hour? Is it really fair to expect the child who is experiencing some sort of domestic difficulties to join in group games when she clearly just wants to be on her own? And why aren't children allowed to shout – you see, if you're playing soldiers and somebody comes after you with a gun, you're hardly likely to want to get close enough to them so that they can hear you whisper, are you?!

So we need to take a reality check in our teams every so often – are our 'rules' really based on the actual likelihood of children coming a cropper, or are they some sort of adult safety net that we don't really need, or are they things that we think are good for children but actually in the context of our setting work *against* children trying to stay within the goalposts? We talked earlier about children whinging – sometimes this can be a good sign for us to realise that our 'rules' need re-looking at! If children are repeatedly getting into trouble for something, then we need to look at that from a child's point of view – is what we are asking of them fair in the first place?

And once we've done our reality check and are sure once more that we are all working to the same bottom line and being fair and consistent, then we can put those goalposts down and get on with our real jobs....it's so much less stressful!

Making rules with children

I have to tell you straight away that I'm really not a big fan of this fad (just in case you didn't pick up the vibes earlier). Lots of reasons...let me take you through a few of the ways that adults generally go about making rules with children and maybe I'll convince you too...

Rules – version no 1 (made by the children, of course)
- No kicking
- No fighting
- No swearing
- No hitting
- Etc, etc, etc....

Sound familiar? Made by the children, written up by the children, put on the wall by the children....and then ignored by the children. Because what this method tends to overlook is the 'natural justice' law applied by children, which goes something like this...

'Rachel, you said that one of your rules was no kicking. Why therefore have you got Johnny on the ground kicking the living daylights out of him?'
'Because he kicked me first!'

or…

'Johnny, it says no swearing up there. Stop swearing.'
'But I was singing – and my favourite rapper swears in his songs all the time!'

Ah yes, there really is no answer to that. Moving on then….

Rules – version no. 2 (the positive ones)

- please walk
- ask adults for help
- be nice to each other

This is what I call 'school rules'. Children have done them before, in their schools, in their classrooms, and when we ask them for 'rules' for our settings, they can chant them out and practically set them to music for us.

Does it help them to know what types of behaviours are expected in our setting? I'm afraid not – because they don't belong to our settings. For example, how can you play football if you are supposed to walk everywhere? What if you don't want to ask adults for help because your mates will think you're a snitch? We also have to be aware that too much prescription in children's lives starts to sound like a sound-track going through their heads – and believe me, it's not something they'd download onto their MP3's, it's more like lift music (and we all know how much attention gets paid to that).

So not appropriate and too ambiguous, I'm afraid... next!

Rules – version no. 3 (the pithy motto)

'Have safe fun!'

Anything strike you about this? There should be two words that bother you – the last two. What if Johnny doesn't want to have 'fun' today – his teacher's been a witch and all he wants to do is sit under a bench and sulk about it? And what if today's the day that Rachel has decided to take that risk she's been working up to and get to the second branch of the tree she's been trying to climb? She won't feel very safe, but she'll probably be quite safe because otherwise she wouldn't try it in the first place. But technically they're breaking the rules and therefore they are getting mixed messages about the types of behaviours appropriate for the setting. So that doesn't do it for us either (apart from which, I also object to it because it makes my setting sound like some ghastly holiday camp.....)

I hope you'll agree with me that all of those ways of making rules lead us right back into those murky behaviour management traps of hesitation, repetition and deviation. You can 'have safe fun', but if your idea of 'fun' is pulling off a spider's legs one by one, forget it – we didn't mean that sort of fun. 'No fighting' – unless it's playfighting, in which case it's ok. And 'please be nice to each other' – except that if you really don't like somebody, it's best just to stay out of their way rather than get into a scrap. Let's face it, if we want children to have even half a chance of getting behaviour 'right', then we really need to make sure that we know what we're talking about in the first place.

Wot, no rules?!

Hang on, hang on – don't panic, we're fixing the goalposts, remember?

Now I could go on here about the fixing and maintaining of boundaries ultimately being the adult's responsibility (because it is) and that we duck that responsibility the minute we start saying to children that they have the 'real' responsibility (because we do). Or I could dwell on the fact that children have quite enough responsibility in their lives nowadays (because they do) at the grand old age of 8 years old, without taking on board the responsibility for the fact that some other kid they don't know - and don't even like - has had ten minutes longer on the PlayStation than 'the agreed time' (because why should they?).

However, for several very good reasons (including the fact that I know you'll do 'making rules' with children and I really don't want you to dabble in any of the dark arts we looked at earlier), I'll curb my inner anarchist and tell you this instead – if you insist on 'doing rules' with kids, do it with positive purpose and the positive intention of helping them to meet the behaviour expectations of the setting, not just because it's the 'in thing' and you can tick a box once you've done it.

Here's how…

The bottom line

Remember that one? When we talked about it earlier we were looking at adults using 'no harm to self, others or property' as a way of getting to grips with deciding when to get involved with children's behaviour. But we can also use it to talk to children about what constitutes 'trouble' in our setting. Yes, yes, I know it's not 'positive', I know it doesn't tell children what to do, but you can see where that sort of fuzzy fluffy stuff gets us from the example above…and anyway, I've got a better idea for how to give kids positive messages about behaviour, but we're not going there until Chapter 3!

How do we want it to be?

Another way of helping children to get the goalposts fixed firmly in their minds is to help them think about the consequences of their behaviour. So instead of asking children what 'rules' they want in their setting, try asking them how they want the setting to be. Then ask them what everybody in the setting (children and adults) need to do to make it like that. And then, if you really feel you must, ask them what you can do if things are not happening in that way.

It's sort of rules, but this process has a positive intention and several positive purposes. First of all, it helps children to understand that 'rules' are there for a purpose – we all have to behave in a certain way if we want to get certain things out of life and help others to do the same. Secondly, it means that when adults need to talk to children about behaviour which doesn't meet expectations, we can link the behaviour to the harm that it does, or is likely to do, not only to others, but also to the child herself. So 'rules' become not just a 'because I say so' (or even 'because you said so' routine), but 'because this is the end result if we don't', conversation.

Remember, if we're helping children to change the way that they behave, then there has to be some motivation for them to do that. The 'behaviour management' process goes something like 'give children a warning and that will put a stop to it'. Behaviour leadership says 'let's find some ways of making it easier for children to get a grip'. We need to make sure that any 'rules' in the setting are appropriate for the children we work with and crystal clear so that children stand a good chance of being able to keep to them.

Consistency (...again)

It takes some practice, especially when we're working in groups, for all of the team to agree on where the goalposts should be fixed and then for all of us to leave

them alone. And the thing to remember about goalposts is that once they are fixed, there are an infinite number of ways of moving about between them.

So teams need to discuss their personal and professional expectations, recognise how they differ and what this means for their professional practice. And they need to do this regularly, because what is realistic for one set of children will be different for the next, and what is likely to cause harm to children is going to vary from setting to setting. Remember, behaviour leadership is about making sure that we are thinking about the children we are working with now – not last years intake, or the place we used to work.

Prepare to leave the goalposts....

So if you're now happy that you've got your goalposts fixed in the right place and are confident enough to leave well alone until you need to review their position again as a team, all we need to do now is to work out the things you can do to help children to stay between them. Piece of cake, Chapter 3!

Chapter 3
Help –
I need somebody....

So now you're focussing on behaviour leadership and helping children to behave in a way that means they can take part, rather than trying to force them to change. And you've got your goalposts firmly fixed and you're not confusing children with vague rules and inconsistent messages any more. Great! So does that mean that all you'll get from now on (from children and adults) is 'perfect' behaviour? No, of course not!

Yes, I know – we try so hard. But we also know, if we think about it logically, that the adult expectation of children 'behaving themselves' just isn't achievable. Because children are children – and either they don't quite get it, or they forget, or they get wrapped up in their play, or they can't deal with strong feelings, or they just don't like it, or it's time to test those boundaries, or they get given a hard time which they resent....there are a million and one reasons why children can't always meet adult expectations, however reasonable and realistic those expectations might be. And seen in the cold light of day, we know that the vast majority of children don't want to be in bother (and those who really think they do need serious help).

So back to our positive intentions and positive purpose – this chapter is about the many things we adults can do to help children to meet the behaviour expectations of the setting. It's not about 'punishment' or 'sanctions' – they belong to behaviour management. It's about the positive intention of reminding children about the

behaviour expectations and helping them to stick to them.

Oh, by the way, just to mention that the title of this chapter was originally referring to the help which children need to meet behaviour expectations. But several adults have told me that that's the way that they feel when faced with children's 'negative' behaviour! So feel free to take it whichever way you like – I won't be testing you later! And if that's the way you feel, then maybe the following will help….

Take a chill pill!

We're going to start with you again – I guess you're getting used to this by now!

The first thing we need to do when helping children to get back between the goalposts is to calm down. Only by being in control yourself can others be in control (and this is especially true when it comes to working with children). In other words, if you are wound up, spitting out words and generally losing it, you can never hope to calm children down and help them to get back within the boundaries of acceptable behaviour in your setting.

So instead of letting your brain go into panic mode (oh no, here we go, he's off again!), try training it to detach itself from the emotion associated with the situation (oh look, how interesting, here comes that type of behaviour, and I've seen that before....). It won't change the way the child behaves in the next few seconds, but it will change the way you approach the situation, which could have a knock-on effect on the way that the child acts next. Wound up children equals wound up adults, and vice-versa, and vice-versa (and no, that last bit wasn't a typo!). We need to take the responsibility for calming negative situations down by making sure that we are calm first.

One of the other ways of making sure that we stay calm, of course, is to make sure that we are only reacting to behaviour that really needs reacting to. We need to keep doing that reality check we talked about in Chapter 2 to make sure that we're only paying attention to stuff that really crosses that bottom line, rather than stuff which just winds us up...

Feelings

If we think about it for a moment, it's pretty easy to see that most, if not all, behaviour has underlying feelings that are associated with them. Feelings can have a powerful effect on the way that we behave – or we can learn to have feelings and to experience different emotions without letting them take over the way that we act.

Children need to experience all forms of emotion (remember, there's no such thing as 'good' and 'bad' feelings). But they also need to learn as they develop that 'feeling' doesn't have to be the same as 'being' – we can have feelings without being run by them. Feelings and behaviour can act as cause and effect to each other

Ahh, the perfect child...
no feelings whatsoever.

– in other words, they get entangled and before you know it, a feeling looks like a behaviour and that behaviour gives rise to other feelings. And so the child ends up being a feeling (for example, 'being happy' or 'being angry'). Sometimes this can have positive effects for the child (and others) - and sometimes it doesn't. One of the old chestnuts of 'behaviour management' is that we should try to understand children's feelings. Personally, I've never been convinced that this does much good (either for us or for the child). Because even if we can understand what the child is feeling (which is going to be a feat when working with a group of, say, forty children and when the majority of us are not trained counsellors), where does that get us in helping children to meet expectations of their behaviour? It doesn't do any harm, of course, for us to understand what's driving a child's behaviour, but it sort of misses the point.

Or to put it another way, just because we 'understand' that Johnny is angry, does that mean that it's ok for him to thump the living daylights out of Fred? No, I think not! The issue here for us adults to take on board is not about understanding, it's about recognising that Johnny's behaviour has been driven by anger so that we can get him to recognise that too. If we help him to separate out the feeling and the being, then maybe next time he feels angry he can choose to do something else with that feeling. But we still also need to deal with the fact that he's hurt somebody!

As children grow and develop, they experience a range of feelings which underlie – and sometimes undermine – the way that they behave. This neither explains, nor excuses, any sort of behaviour, but it does help us to remember that this is a natural part of growing up and part of a whole process which we can support. One of the ways that we can do this is by naming feelings for children, to help them to separate out the feeling from the being.

So for example, a girl skipping down a school corridor (when the 'rule' is that she should walk) may feel happy that she is going home, excited about going to her after-school club, or perhaps pleased about the fact that her teacher has just told her something good about herself. This is a good thing – she's feeling happy, and it is important to acknowledge that for the child. And yet, of course, there may be perfectly valid reasons why she should walk instead of skipping. But before she gets told not to skip and to walk, she needs to know that feeling happy is ok (it's just the behaviour that isn't). So instead of 'Jemima, I've told you before not to skip here', we need to say something like 'Jemima, you look happy today, that's great! But instead of skipping along the corridor, how about you give us a huge smile instead?'

Talking to children

We use an awful lot of verbal communication with children about their behaviour, but if we really think about it and are honest with ourselves, quite a lot of it serves a different purpose to that of helping children to stay between those goalposts; it helps us adults to vent our frustration, or it makes us feel like we're in control, or it puts inappropriate responsibility onto children. None of these actually help children to know what's expected of them in the setting, which should of course be the focus of all our communication with children about their behaviour.

The trouble with 'negative' behaviour is that it can breed negative communication in adults. For example;

How many times have I told you?

Er, six actually.

❖ 'I've told you before/a thousand times/last week'.
Well, it obviously didn't work then, so saying that is not going to help the child in the here and now, is it?

❖ 'Don't you know that..'
Obviously not, or if they did, they've chosen not to know for some reason, so whether they know or not isn't the issue, right?

❖ 'Can you tell me why you kicked Johnny/bit
   Jemima/made the budgie fall off his perch?'
This one always makes me smile. Just what are we
adults expecting here – a long, thoughtful analysis from
an 5-year old as to why they've just acted irrationally
and thoughtlessly? You see, if they knew why they were
doing it in the first place, they probably wouldn't have
done it – after all, what child wants to get into the sorts
of bother that this sort of behaviour will inevitably heap
onto them?

What are you doing that for?

The other problem with the 'why did you do that' variety of question is that we are likely to get an answer such as 'cos I felt like it' (or worse) – and where do you go from there?

So instead of getting bogged down in asking them why, or getting sidetracked into other issues, here's a simple, no-blame-no-shame, positive way of communicating the fact that children have crossed the line;

1. Tell them 'no'

Now I know that the word 'no' has been much frowned on in many areas of working with children. But I'm not sure why. Children need a clear message that a particular behaviour is not acceptable. Asking them 'why' merely implies interest, or, even worse, that you know they've done wrong and there will be merry hell to pay once you've 'had a bit of a chat'. Children need to be clearly reminded about the goalposts – not involved in a 10-minute discourse on behaviour philosophy.

Remember too, that for children who are really worked up and even out of control, then they need you to re-fix those goalposts for them. If they've lost the plot, then we're the ones who have to try and help them find it again – not push them so far out of their normal behaviour patterns that it feels like they're never coming back, because that will really result in some behaviour to worry about, trust me!

2. Tell them why not

Give them a reason for why the behaviour is unacceptable – but make sure it is based in fact. This does not include 'because I told you yesterday', or any accusations that are likely to damage the child's self-esteem, eg, 'you're/that's really stupid'. The information we give needs to be focussed on helping the child to understand the consequences of that particular action (eg, you'll hurt yourself/break the table etc).

3. Tell them what to do instead

This stage should also involve naming feelings which may have caused the child to lose the boundary in the first place. 'I can see you're cross about losing the game – but instead of taking it out on the table, have a go at thumping those cushions instead.'

4. Give them positive attention for positive behaviour.

'I see you gave those cushions a real good bashing earlier – are you feeling better now?' Please note – not 'thank you for thumping the cushions'. Why not? Because that simply rewards the child for doing what they were told by an adult. Positive attention helps children to think for themselves and take responsibility for their own behaviour. In this case, the link is made for the child between thumping the cushion and feeling better. Maybe they could use that information in the future to deal with anger.

And while we're on the subject...

...we'll just deal with some other unhelpful habits we adults have when communicating with children about their behaviour. There's really no polite way to put this, so could we please all just take the pledge to cease;

❖ finger wagging
❖ sarcasm
❖ talking at children, rather than talking to them
❖ harping on about what a pain the child was yesterday/last week/last year(!)
❖ making children say they're sorry (they're probably not and if they do say it they're only doing it to get you off their case, so what's the point?)
❖ shouting

Now say you're sorry...

Thanks – you know it makes sense!

Early intervention techniques

Because we spend so much time observing children, we know when they are about to lose it. And as our focus for intervention is to help them to stay within the goalposts of the setting, here's some techniques that we can use to help children so that they don't have to lose it….

❖ *Distraction* – taking the child's mind off what's about to go wrong and onto something else

❖ *Limiting equipment access* – for one session only and for the child who is struggling only (not all of them, that isn't fair!)

❖ *Hurdle help* – asking the child if they need some help with the next bit to get them over whatever is about to cause them aggro

❖ *Reminders* – telling children that it seems that they have 'forgotten' whatever the boundary is you need them to remember and explaining again what it is they need to do

❖ *Planned ignoring* – the whole team decides that a particular behaviour is being produced to attract negative attention from adults so decide not to pay any attention to the child when they act in that way (unless, of course, the child's behaviour is going to cause some harm, in which case this is not an appropriate adult response!)

❖ *Proximity* – sometimes just wandering in the direction of a child will be enough of a signal that they are in danger of moving the wrong side of the goalposts. And sometimes the physical presence is quite enough – you don't even need to look in their direction!

❖ *Direct appeal* – my favourite with older kids – simply telling them that you really need them to do whatever because… (and link to the consequences as we talked about in Chapter 2).

Positive attention

It will come as no surprise to you by now when I say that positive attention is more likely to result in positive behaviour. Not guaranteed, obviously, as kids will still have bad days and bad moods and hormones and sulks and fall-outs with their best mates…but 'more likely' is good enough for me!

Sometimes adults get so carried away with what they need to achieve, or what has to happen in the setting, that they forget the simple things which encourage positive behaviour in return – saying hello, asking children what sort of day they've had, playing with them…It's so easy to get distracted by the things that need doing, the kids that are 'playing up', other adult agendas…and then we wonder why the children get stressed out too! We said in Chapter 1 that we shouldn't be permanently on the look-out for 'bad' behaviour - we should instead keep our eyes peeled for the every day positive stuff which children do, without fuss or drama, and give them positive attention for that.

It's also important to spread good news – if you work with parents, then the temptation is to make sure we pass on the news about what a pain in the neck Johnny has been today. Can we truthfully say that we always put as much effort into making sure that we catch the carers of Fred, who has been an absolute angel?

Remember that positive attention means the time that we spend with children each day, talking about what they want to talk about, showing an interest in who they are, having a laugh and a joke with them. Positive attention does not mean doing star charts or any other form of 'behaviour bribery' – stickers, certificates, reward systems with points… you'll get my drift.

And yes, of course I realise that these have been one of

the last beastions (that was originally a typo, but I thought it was rather appropriate, so I've left it in!) of the behaviour management approach. If all else fails, resort to coercing children into doing what we want them to do through material gains. And if the material gains on offer aren't enough, or lose their appeal, then do it even more, make the rewards bigger, have more award ceremonies....If we're not careful, we're soon all going to end up spending all of our time administering these cumbersome and extremely limited systems, instead of actually spending time with the kids.

Behaviour leadership starts with the positive intention that the goalposts are fixed in a reasonable and realistic position and it's entirely possible and desirable for everybody to stay somewhere in-between them. Of course we accept that some of us in the setting might need some help every now and again, but generally speaking the expectations are positive and we'd all like to keep it that way. We don't need to make a fuss about 'good' behaviour because the rewards that we all get from children and adults staying between those goalposts are reward enough in themselves – a happy atmosphere, space for children to be themselves, time and attention from chilled adults who are pleased to be spending time with the children they are working with. Reward systems, ceremonies etc start with a negative intention – they give the rather unfortunate message to the children that we are so convinced that they are not going to meet the behaviour expectations that we have to make a huge fuss about it when they do.

People who work with younger children often object at this point, saying that younger children like the reward systems and the smiley dinosaur stickers. Sorry folks, that just sort of proves my point really, doesn't it? You can bribe younger children with certificates and stickers, or even chocolate spread sandwiches for that matter, but we know that none of them will do them any good in the long run. Because none of those things help children to understand that actions are linked to consequences and all types of behaviour have intrinsic long-term effects for ourselves and others. So we need to hang onto our positive intentions and positive purpose and place those short-term quick fix anti-solutions firmly on that bonfire....

Thanks – but no thanks....

From elsewhere out of the depths of 'behaviour management' came that rather peculiar 'technique' of 'praising children'. And that has generally come to mean 'thanking' children – as in, thanks for hanging your coat up, thanks for tidying up, and so on. I guess it is a form of positive attention - at least we're all noticing that children are staying between the goalposts and telling them so — but it seems to have turned into a bit of a mantra, a bit of a routine. Or as one child said to a playworker in an after school club a few weeks back as she was putting chairs away, 'Yeah yeah, don't bother to thank me, I'm doing it anyway.' Has 'praising' and 'thanking' children just become another form of behaviour bribery?

Children who feel good about themselves and who get lots of positive attention from adults have less need to test behaviour boundaries and try to get any sort of attention by producing the type of behaviour which is guaranteed to make adults sit up and take notice. (I might have mentioned this earlier but it's worth repeating, don't you think?!) So let's give children a lot of positive attention for who they are, not just what they do (especially if that only turns out to be the sort of behaviour which pleases adults…). By all means we can thank them for doing stuff, but let's also feed their sense of well-being by telling them that they are funny, clever, patient, kind, brave — in other words, we need to make sure that we are praising well-being as much, if not more than, well-doing!

Banning labels

Any sort of labels which are attached to children will get in the way of them being able to achieve the behaviour expectations of the setting. A child who already 'knows' that they are 'bad' or 'good' will be more likely to act in accordance with their label – and if we've let them know (however subtly) that they are 'a trouble-maker', then this doesn't leave them much room

for manoeuvre, does it? Similarly, we may find that children who have been labelled as 'good' by adults decide that they have *more* than enough room for manoeuvre now that everybody knows what an angel they are!

Let's not limit potential with labels – kids are kids, with the whole range of behaviour at their disposal. To put labels on them, or to accept other people's labels, or even to pass kids on with labels attached like Paddington Bear, is just not fair on the child. After all, most of us have been in the situation where Rachel has come from her school to the playbus with, apparently, 'pain' tattooed across her forehead. However, on the playbus Rachel is one of the most friendly, helpful children that you could ever hope to meet.

And just a final word about labels – children have a remarkable knack of picking up on the fact that adults think badly of them, even if those adults have never said a word to anybody. This doesn't help children to meet behaviour expectations, so we need to get rid of those labels and treat children like children, rather than packages.

So, there you go. Loads of different ways to help children to recognise and stay within the goalposts of your setting, and all starting with the positive intention and positive purpose of wanting children to be able to achieve the behaviour expectations of the setting.

And remember – it all starts with you...

And finally...

Just before we part company, I need you to think about 'little Johnny', to whom some of you will have said a fond farewell at the start of the book.

Now we've reached the end of the book, please do feel free to think about him/her again – but only if you promise me one thing...

...that when you think about him from now on, you will not think about what you are going to do *with* him (or even *to* him!), but what you are going to do *for* him.

Try it – I can't promise you it will be the answer, but I can promise that it will make a difference – for both of you.

THE LEARNING CENTRE
STANMORE COLLEGE
HARROW HA7 4BQ
TEL:020 8420 7730

00022202